WHEN
CLOWNS
ATTACK

CHUCK SAMBUCHINO

WHEN
CLOWNS
ATTACK

A Guide to the
Scariest People on Earth

TEN SPEED PRESS
Berkeley

3: DEFEND

4: PROTECT

"Parents are all like, 'Aren't the clowns funny, Johnny?' and Johnny's like 'No! Get me the hell outta here! These people are all crazy!'"

—STEPHEN KING

INTRODUCTION

"Step right up. Come one, come all." What you read in these pages just might save your life.

Right now, in every nation around the globe, the greatest danger isn't nuclear proliferation or the possibility of World War III. It is, in fact, *clowns*. I know what you're thinking—sure, these red-nosed jokers are creepy, but they're not really dangerous, and all those rumors about clowns and crime (such as the size-22 shoe prints found near where they last saw Jimmy Hoffa) are just the sensational drivel of conspiracy theorists.

Those kinds of naïve misconceptions are exactly what people think right before they get stabbed in a neighborhood controlled by clown gangs.

The truth is, while plenty of these bozos are capable of only acts such as petty theft right before they drunkenly pee their pants, too many others commit much worse crimes—especially if you provoke them. Clowns are everywhere, both in costume and in plainclothes, and if you encounter one *mano a clowno*, your best-case outcome is a traumatized child (and adult); the worst is loss of loot, limb, or life.

For decades these performers have haunted us—at Halloween fright fests, in the depths of carnival funhouses, and in Batman movies. All the while, we wonder what the heck they're hiding in those enormous shoes. *Weapons? Booze? A syringe?* Probably all three—we just don't know. We generally don't know *anything* about a clown—hence our fear of them. And after decades of their multiplying unchecked and engaging in a public relations campaign to make us believe they're symbols of jollity and happiness, our planet now confronts a full-blown bozo epidemic.

It's with all this in mind that I, founder of the anti-clown group Red Nose Alert, sat down to compose this life-saving guide. Both my grandfathers suffered assaults at the hands of deranged jokers years ago, so I learned from a young age that clowns are just as violent and demented as we've suspected. We at Red Nose Alert want to share our knowledge with you before it's too late.

However evil you may already think these performers are, they're worse. Some will assault bystanders for no reason; others are working with much grander goals in mind. Want details? Brace yourself. Clown cartels control illicit drug distribution channels, black-market organ sales, and pantaloon outlet stores in every major city worldwide. To keep their numbers high, they abduct and brainwash children to join their polka-dotted ranks. And once they've collected enough money, children, and helium, they'll realize their ultimate goal of world domination—where brutal "clown law" is absolute and final.

Have you ever wondered why clowns eat so many Twinkies? It's because these cream-filled snacks can survive a nuclear blast, and clowns are convinced that if they consume enough Twinkies, no amount of radiation will be able to stop them. After the nuclear fallout, all that will be left are cockroaches and clowns—which was exactly their plan all along. Meanwhile, every year, while the public continues to believe that clowns are happy, peppy people at best, and a little creepy but harmless at worst, they inch that much closer to the front door and your toddler.

But fear not. Now that you are aware of the imminent danger, you're much safer than you were sixty seconds ago. The next thing you can do is rip up those tickets to the circus and then sit down to learn everything you can about protecting yourself and your family. Do you know how to use a banana peel or exploding cigar to stop a group of approaching jokers? How shoe color designates clown gang rankings? We will teach you all that and more.

In these pages, you'll learn everything you need to know about clown anatomy and attire, clown props, locations and gatherings of clowns, clown attacks, infamous clowns (serial killer John Wayne Gacy, anyone?), and more. So what you need to do now is go to the window and listen for circus music or any *hyuk-hyuk* laughter. Peer out into the street to check for unicycle graffiti symbols or plainclothes clown gangsters selling laughing gas right there in broad daylight. If it's all clear, then you're safe—for now. Deadbolt the doors and settle in. This book will no doubt save your skin.

1

ASSESS

Feel the Fear

WHY CLOWNS FRIGHTEN PEOPLE

The pro-clown lobby has recently led a public relations effort to dismiss fear of clowns—"coulrophobia"—as an "irrational fear" or "absurd phobia." But don't be fooled. People are innately afraid because they *should* be. Clowns thrive on creating discomfort, disruption, fear, and chaos—and we're supposed to be OK with this madness simply because they do it with a smile.

In this chapter, you will find the seven reasons we fear clowns. Once you study these reasons, you'll understand that your trepidation is natural and warranted—and you'll be ready to learn more about protecting yourself in the future.

1. YOU NEVER KNOW THEIR REAL NAMES. When a clown introduces himself to you, he explains that his name is "Scooter!!" and that he lives "at the circus with other fun, magical people!!" But of course these are both lies. Nothing about a clown's introduction or interaction with you is genuine. They have a false face and a false name and a false backstory—making them completely impossible to believe—and more important, impossible for police to locate. Plus, a large percentage of clown names are actually code names for hard drugs.

DECODING COMMON CLOWN NAMES

+ **STITCHES**: They claim that this name refers to how they'll make you laugh ("have you in stitches"), but it actually refers to how they'll *literally* have you in stitches after an attack. Generally, the ones who've seen the most violence adopt this nickname.

+ **HAPPY**: Any joker with this name is hooked on ecstasy.

+ **POWDER**: Standard nickname for a cocaine-dealing clown.

+ **ANGEL**: Although it's so obviously code for angel dust (PCP), you commonly find clowns named Angel at little girls' birthday and princess parties.

+ **FUZZY**: Clowns get this sobriquet because of their love of weed, kilos of which they can stash in those baggy pants.

+ **SUNSHINE**: Shortened name is code for "yellow sunshine" or "orange sunshine"—both variants of LSD. That bright swirly tie they always wear? Loaded and entirely lickable.

+ **KIBBLES**: Kibbles (or "Kib-Daddy," as he prefers to be called) is your crack cocaine dealer of the mix. Commonly seen juggling flaming torches, this bozo always has a light.

+ **SNIFF/SNIFFLES**: Also a nickname for cocaine-loving bozos. Though where Powder traffics in uncut, Sniffles usually plies street-grade stuff know as "Sweet & Low."

+ **GIGGLES**: Master of laughing gas/nitrous oxide. Brought in when civilians need subduing. Rarely seen without canisters and bags of balloons.

2. **THEY GO STRAIGHT FOR THE CHILDREN.** If you were at a park and a stranger walked right up to your kids and started handing them candy, I'm guessing you would either call 911 or slug him across his *Dateline* predator face. Yet this behavior is a clown's everyday M.O. Not only do clowns head straight for everyone's offspring, they also pass around a bevy of snacks and sugary treats. Best-case scenario: a wired kid. Worst case: the cops are putting out an Amber Alert for your little one. The scary reality is that almost all clowns are men, so breeding large numbers is a centuries-old challenge for the community. Their twisted solution is to grab orphans, street kids, and little ones who wander a little too far away from the minivan, to indoctrinate them into the clowning lifestyle and world.

3. **THEY SEEM IMPERVIOUS TO PAIN OR INJURY.** Clowns get hit on the head with a mallet, attacked down the pants with fire extinguishers, and slammed in the face with countless pies in metal tins, only to remain . . . perfectly functional. This isn't slapstick humor; it's borderline *superpowers.* But since there is no such thing as superpowers, we must naturally assume this comes from ingesting PCP, a narcotic known to dull the nerves and cause users to feel no sensation, even when breaking a bone.

4. **EVERYTHING ABOUT THEM IS UNNATURAL.** Think about it. Everything that clowns do is abnormal, unsanctioned behavior, and even their very appearance is deviant. For instance:

+ **Their hat?** Never the right size. Way too large or way too small.

+ **Their skin tone?** Never a natural human color.

+ **Their pants?** Creepily loose. They could be hiding anything from a sharpened spatula to a bazooka inside those bad boys.

+ **Their shoes?** Enormous and way too heavy. It takes just one stomp to snap a femur, and only three well-placed stomps to crush a man to death.

+ **Their laughter?** Saying "Hyuk-hyuk!" is in no way normal. Recently, a Scottish scholar discovered the word hyuk has its roots in an Old English verb for "to stab." So the next time you hear a party clown say "I hyuked the last guy who didn't give me a tip," give that joker a tip — seriously.

+ **Their transportation?** Unicycles are dangerous, and clown cars are death traps that defy the laws of physics. .

+ **Their hair?** Never a natural color, shape, or size. More often than not, it's a clown-fro that looks like a pom-pom stolen from a local high school cheerleader.

5. **THEY DO WHATEVER THEY WANT, WITH NO
CONSEQUENCES.** Because clowns occupy a wacky world
and profession, they think they're not subject to the same
rules the rest of us are—and that is truly terrifying. If
a clown wants to come up to you and give you an over-
the-head wedgie, he'll do just that. If a clown wants to
embarrass you in front of your date and slap you in the face
with cotton candy or a giant balloon monkey, he'll do just
that. And all of these things are apparently OK—simply
because clowns somehow have us all believing that the rules
of civilized society, and even the laws of a nation, do not
apply to them.

6. **THEY HIDE THEIR TRUE NUMBERS.** "Clowns are pack
hunters," says Dr. Ryan McElvy, circus arts researcher at
Columbia University. "You may think a car that just pulled
up has four or even five clowns squeezed into it, only to see
fifteen pop out. All indicators point to clown troupes being
a cover for criminal activities. Clowns have adopted gang
behavior in the last fifty years. You insult one guy, and the
next minute you're surrounded by a Cirque du Soleil
from hell, all brandishing baseball bats."

7. OUR INSTINCTS TELL US THAT THEY'RE FREAKING WEIRD AND SHOULD BE AVOIDED. Besides fear of heights, do you know the most common fear held by the public? It isn't fear of snakes, death, public speaking, or even an uncontained zombie virus. It is, of course, fear of clowns. You may think you're the only one who gets spooked by a rainbow wig, but the truth is that fear of clowns is widespread. For instance, in a recent survey about preferences for a hospital redesign, out of 250 children ages four to sixteen, every single one expressed fear or dislike of clown imagery. Even when uninformed about clowns' nefarious nature, innocent children have a healthy fear of them. This is clear evidence of evolution: as the human body has now adapted to sense a zany circus predator and go into defense mode without prompting from others.

THE MENTAL INSTABILITY OF CLOWNS

To understand why clowns are so dangerous, you must study the journey of a clown. Some are certifiable before they ever even put on face paint. Others were somewhere on the spectrum of normal until they become a bozo, but the creepy ways of clowning, year after year, inevitably take their mental toll. After talking with dozens of former jokers, investigators began to see an alarming pattern of difficult life experiences that too often tip a clown into madness, crime, and danger:

+ **Clowns are repeatedly injured.** Although they show no outward sign of pain or harm, every day for years and years they sustain injuries, be it a bruised noggin from juggling to singed eyebrows from a fire gag gone wrong. And when they're seriously hurt during a performance, everyone thinks it's a joke and laughs at them. That's why they've found ways to hide or even suppress the pain—mostly handfuls of oxycodone—but they still can't escape the mental toll.

+ **Clowns are under immense pressure to always draw a laugh.** You think high-pressure sales is tough, with its quotas and cold calling? Try being a comedian for several hours a day, seven days a week. If you don't get the audience chuckling, your big-top boss withholds your paycheck faster than you can say "Vaudeville is dead."

◆ **Even when clowns get paid, it's usually crap wages.**
Imagine: after exhausting, twelve-hour days in insane heat,
you get your weekly paycheck of . . . $180. You'd steal, too,
and you'd probably succumb to the allure of drugs to kill the
sadness—just like they do. Clowns learn how to pickpocket
and grift early in their careers, because too often it's the
only way to put food in their big red mouths.

◆ **Clowns are no longer the hottest show in town.** Back in the
1800s, the circus was the biggest form of entertainment in
the world. Clowns were called artists—or better yet, *artistes*.
These glory days of yesteryear are long past. The modern
clown hates his irrelevance. The only kind of artist he is in
today's world is a *con* artist.

◆ **Clowns almost never get the girls.** Most clowns are men,
and these particular men are at the bottom of the circus
groupie food chain. The guy who rides the motorcycle
in the circular cage gets dates. The guy who gets shot out
of a cannon gets dates. But the clown? He goes back to
his trailer alone. The loneliness can make a man do crazy
things, such as conspire to establish a New World Order
of Clowns in which *he* will call the shots and attract all
the ladies.

◆ **Clowns are shunned if they improve or evolve their act.**
As the twentieth century progressed, progressive clowns
tried incorporating new elements, such as literary

references and social themes, only to find themselves ignored and broke. No one wanted a new, sophisticated array of japery. They wanted to see a clown go haywire after his butt was lit on fire. This means clowns are forced to do the same gags, day in and day out—forever. This lack of variety drives clowns to madness.

+ **The clown's function is to fail.** What kind of job has daily goals that include being mocked, failing repeatedly, and demonstrating your own incompetence? Clowning—that's what kind. Over time, this leads to psychotic disorders, hallucinations, and just downright bitterness and contempt for normal people.

After understanding how a clown's screws can slowly come loose, you may be inclined to feel sympathy for them. As kind as this inclination may be, it makes you even more vulnerable for future attacks. This guide's next part—Analyze: Breaking Down a Clown—will show you all the means they have to attack.

And we must acknowledge here that there are indeed a small percentage of clowns (it's believed to be around 8 percent) who do not pose any type of threat. These are kooky, oddball performers who were drawn to the profession because of altruism. But that 8 percent aside, we still urge you to adopt our Red Nose Alert mantra of "There's no such thing as a good clown." Because even if a bozo starts out friendly and harmless, the consequences of living the clown life will likely drive him off a mental cliff. And we'd put our money on the 92-percent chance that when you go toe-to-toe with Bozo, you'll find that he has quite a few bats in the belfry.

CLOWN INFLUENCE THROUGHOUT HISTORY

THE TEN PLAGUES OF EGYPT
(FOURTEENTH CENTURY BCE)

Historical theologians have long insisted there were actually eleven plagues, not ten. The missing plague (which actually came seventh) was hordes of unfunny clowns descending on Egypt with honker horns and bad jokes. The original biblical text is as follows:

This is what the LORD, the God of the Hebrews says: Let my people go, so that they may worship me. If you do not, the hand of the LORD will bring about countless painted faces from the land you will one day call France—to ruin your world with bland humor and stupid, pointless gags. Their juggling shall block out the sun.

It's believed this plague was excised from the Bible because the people of Egypt were more confused than anything else, having possibly never seen a clown or jester before. (God works in mysterious ways.) Plus, the clown invasion was little more than a horrendous nuisance—making it the unquestionable dud of all the plagues.

THE CRUSADES (1095)

Clowns were behind it all. It all comes down to the fact that Italian clowns during the Middle Ages weren't getting any dates—simple as that. No one wanted to marry these imbeciles or even get near them, so the country's clowning community came up with an intricate and mischievous plan. They spread rumors to high-ranking officials of the Roman Catholic Church that non-Christian areas in the Middle East could easily be overtaken and converted to the religion. The Church, believing this would be an easy task ("a slam dunk" was the exact phrase Pope Urban II used), sent hundreds of thousands of men to "take back" the Holy Land. With virtually all able-bodied men gone from Italy during the next decade, the clowns and jesters left behind—most deemed "way too freaking weird for military service"—were the big men on campus by default and finally attracted the notice of attention-starved women. Meanwhile, at least one million people died during the Crusades.

THE GREAT CHICAGO FIRE (1871)

The blaze, which left a large portion of the city's population homeless, was not started by a cow. In fact, it was started by Tatters the Clown, who held a grudge against the O'Leary family after performing at a party for their two-year-old son. Since the O'Learys had never hired a clown before, they were unaware that Tatters would expect a hefty tip at the end of the party. When he was not given a tip, he went to the O'Leary's barn later that night and committed arson, unaware that his fiery vengeance would quickly spread to almost half the city. The police reports show that Tatters later confessed after a several-day drinking bender, but the officers thought the admission was a gag and simply laughed. As Tatters left the station examining the two bits (twenty-five cents) the cops had thrown to him as they laughed, only then did he realize he'd finally gotten his tip.

Continues on page 23

THE SINKING OF THE RMS *TITANIC* (1912)

Although popular wisdom has it that the lookouts for Titanic spotted the iceberg with little *time to spare,* there was indeed *time to spare.* They radioed the warning quickly to the bridge, and word was further relayed down to the engine room to alter the turbines and turn the ship. But it took an extra 120 seconds for the engine room workers to hear the message, because they were watching two intoxicated clowns duke it out in a fight. The wealthy guests on the boat were entertained by orchestras, but *Titanic's* management had opted to spring for only two cheap clowns to entertain the overworked engine room workers. During the first few nights of the voyage, no one in the engine rooms paid attention to the jokers, prompting each of them, independently, to come down to the turbines very drunk late in the evening of April 14. When they crossed paths, an accidental bump turned into a bitter shove turned into a flurry of haymaker punches. Unintentionally, the clowns finally gave the engine room workers something interesting to look at, so the workers left their stations to watch the pair of obliterated clowns pulverize each other. This happened at the worst possible moment, as the directional orders from the bridge went unheeded for two minutes. In the end, the boat turned too little and too late, and *Titanic* sank, resulting in the death of 1,500 people (and though we'd like to think both clowns went down with the ship, this is sadly unconfirmed).

HOW TO CONNECT
WITH OTHER COULROPHOBES

While you are avoiding clowns, it's nice to make friends who are as vehemently anti-clown as you are. One secret way to do this (under the radar of snooping clowns), when in a public situation, is to nonchalantly say *"Mors est nebulo"* (Latin for "Death to clowns"). This phrase was found on a centuries-old European parchment found in Greece. Though the author of the document and words are unknown, it's probable that whoever created the document was part of the first anti-clown secret society on record. That's why, to this day, all coulrophobes use *Mors est nebulo* as a calling card to see if any other like-minded heroes are standing around. This is how we quietly meet and network with one another, while not drawing the attention of clown sympathizers at the NSA.

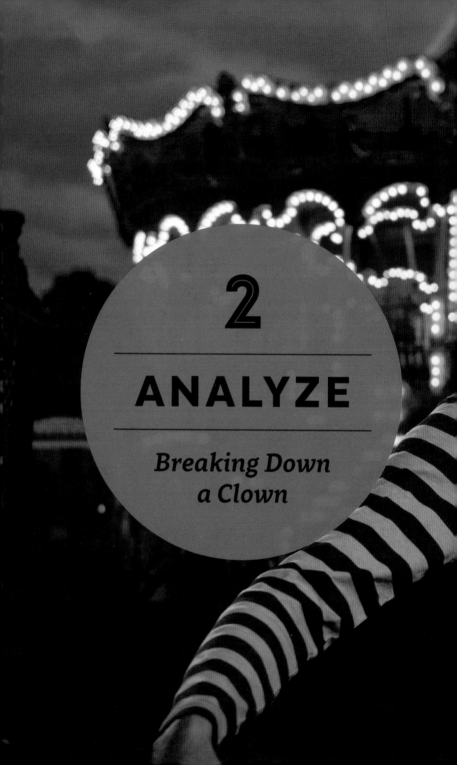

2

ANALYZE

*Breaking Down
a Clown*

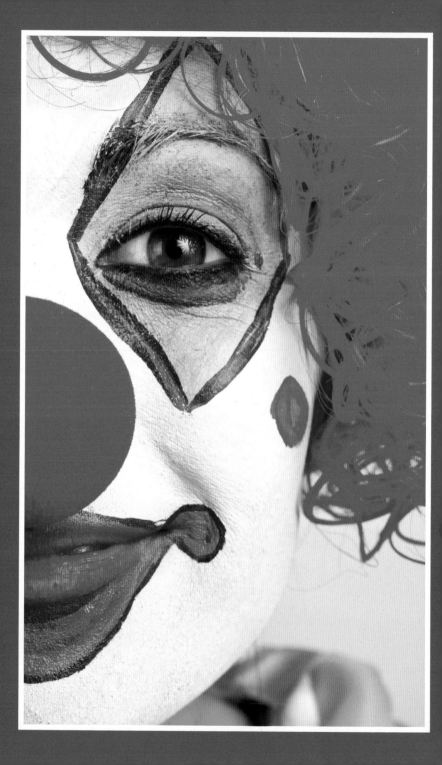

TYPES OF CLOWNS

While virtually all clowns pose some type of danger or risk to your health and retirement savings, they're not all the same. You need to fully understand the different types of jokers out there so you can identify their breed quickly to assess their weaknesses in a fight and safeguard your valuables.

The Party Clown

The basics: Frequently found at children's parties, usually hired by some tone-deaf elderly relative who misguidedly thinks that kids actually like clowns. This breed is typically an apprentice who can't hack the big tent. He is usually drunk, and often he will scream, at no one in particular, *"You think you're better'n me?!?"* A party clown's tricks are simple and lame — a few amateur balloon animals occupy the children, while parents gather by the wine and cheese to concur that the entertainer smells like cheap tequila.

Dangerous because: While everyone at the party is having a ball discussing the "sad bozo," the house and valuables are unguarded. Low-danger party clowns are typically amateur con men who sell themselves cheap to McMansion birthday parties, while a circus worker accomplice sneaks into the house to quietly pocket the silver and prescription drugs. However, a master party clown, though rare, is one of the most dangerous jokers around. He's the sober snake charmer who throws candy and Sacagawea dollars all over the yard to create chaos and misdirection while he kidnaps a youngster to be brainwashed and inducted into clowndom and circus life forever. Scary stuff.

Weaknesses: A party clown's weaknesses are self-inflicted. Because the lower-level ones are inebriated 97 percent of the time (according to numerous official studies), they quickly end up on the radar of protective parents. It's not easy to steal a Rolex when you're seriously impaired *and* all the dads at the party are watching you like hawks.

The Circus Clown

The basics: The modern-day circus clown—a "whiteface" whose origins can be traced back to Italian *commedia dell'arte*—is perhaps the most well-known of the clown archetypes. The circus clown is a crafty performer and the most talented of his ilk. These are the clowns who can tie a huge bowtie in less than ten seconds, the ones who buy top-of-the-line oversize clown pants to best hide bowling pins and tear gas canisters. They are typically more serious and sophisticated (read: less creepy but more dangerous) than other categories of joker.

Dangerous because: The whiteface prides himself on performing perilous acts *behind the scenes*. For example, they often train dangerous circus animals to do the dirty work and become guard animals for clown mafia *capos*. They also are big into white-collar crime ("ruffled collar crime"), including scams that range from extortion to insurance fraud. A whiteface is clever enough to "mistakenly" make a seemingly impossible bet (such as juggle five bowling pins at once), but then, *surprise!* he is able to perform the task and runs away with your money before you can call him a hustler. But most of all, the whiteface is dangerous because his onstage public persona—seen at large circus events—is a white*wash*. As the most public clown, he generally portrays himself as well behaved and kind, serving as a twisted public relations effort for the entire treacherous circus community.

Weaknesses: As the whiteface is the most cultured of his kind and his strengths are mostly intellectual, he is not a tough opponent physically. So if you feel like you just got conned out of a bet, there's a good chance you will be able to deck the S.O.B. and get your money back. Just be aware that a whiteface may have some protection around to combat this very problem—say, or a protective white tiger nearby that kills on command.

The Street Clown

The basics: Easily the most unpredictable of the breeds, a street clown performs without certification or supervision. These crazy clowns are commonly found in urban downtown areas and tourist districts, where they do any number of things to attract a crowd and overuse a laugh box: juggling, flame throwing, and crowd-sourced balancing acts. Street clowns can have bizarre behaviors, too. They're the ones who will lick your face for a laugh or physically bully you into coughing up a tip. If they do work with an accomplice, it's someone in plainface—a plant working the crowd—who spots wealthy people and slips tracking devices into their pockets. Then they'll track those poor S.O.B.s' movements home so they know which house to burgle later that week.

Dangerous because: Bozos with mental issues or God complexes end up as street clowns more often than not. And it's almost always a street clown who drives that suspicious-looking ice cream truck around the neighborhood at night, peddling drugs and crappy circus music CDs. Street clowns have serious self-worth issues, having not passed muster to perform under the big top nor even at children's parties. This means you could easily insult them without trying—and find yourself on the receiving end of a mallet to the face.

Weaknesses: If you ever find yourself in a volatile situation with a street clown, yell, "Look! They're having circus tryouts over there!" and point somewhere. The street clown will no doubt stop fighting you and awkwardly gallop in the direction you pointed. He's so desperate to get hired at a true three-ring circus that your argument becomes small potatoes instantly.

The Tramp or Hobo

The basics: A uniquely American clown; some believe they originated with the hobos who rode the rails during the Great Depression. Today's classic tramp clown look includes a sooty face with white around the eyes and mouth. You'll spot tramp clowns easily because they refuse to smile, look like they just stepped out of a John Steinbeck poverty nightmare, and often have fewer teeth then a meth junkie.

Dangerous because: While they are not known for master pickpocketing skills (unlike their more common whiteface and street clown brethren), they have mastered the art of encouraging donations with their sad-sack looks. In fact, a key danger in encountering a professional hobo is that he's so depressing that you just want to freaking kill yourself. (Though if you did, he'd swoop in like a vulture and rifle through the pockets on your still-warm body.)

Weaknesses: The tramp is a fragile being. If you're cornered by one, insult his lack of either friends or a meaningful direction in life. This will quickly force the clown to break down crying and give you room to escape with your health and personal effects intact.

The Dunking Booth Clown

The basics: A specialized subspecies most often found at carnivals, these clowns are mean-spirited jerk-faces— sadomasochistic foes desirous of both receiving and giving punishment. Former U.S. Representative Eve Potter, who chaired the Subcommittee on Carnival Dangers, says, "Because the dunking booth clown is considered volatile, he's usually in a cage. When you hit the target and he gets dunked, he falls into a bath that's sometimes full of industrial canal water— loaded with chemical runoff. Carnival administrators do this to keep a dunking booth clown bats**t crazy and spewing insults at a rapid-fire. I saw hidden camera footage that confirmed how dunking booth clowns are kept under lock and key off hours because even other clowns fear them."

Dangerous because: Dunking booth clowns cannot be bargained or reasoned with. If one of them gets loose and is sitting next to you at a sports bar, then you *are* getting into a fight, and he *will* bite you during the fight.

Weaknesses: None. He's crazy. If you see one, get the hell out of there.

The Cirque du Soleil "Clown"

The basics: The Cirque "clown" isn't considered a real clown in today's society, as he is the only breed of joker known to *not* incorporate theft, violence, or narcotics into his daily lifestyle. That said, the problem is that he's incredibly artsy and pretentious, which makes him virtually intolerable. *And* he usually speaks in French, and only in metaphors, so if you're not up on your Romance languages it can be hard to differentiate a cutting insult from idle chitchat.

Dangerous because: The Cirque clown's kind of attack—the psychological—is often overlooked but particularly dangerous. Between his nose-in-the-air, lightning-fast miming and his sick pleasure in the fact that you don't *get* his historical artistic references, he can drive you so stark raving mad that you just open-palm smack him right there in the casino lobby. And then you're in jail for assault—and who controls the jail crime syndicates? The damn clowns. So since this breed is technically considered an ally of the anti-clown community, it's best to let them have their insults and keep walking.

Weaknesses: If you want to antagonize a Cirque, all you have to do is take some potshots at Marcel Proust or even the metric system, then watch his rage trigger an aneurysm. Or offer him a crepe to get him to stop whatever annoying thing he's doing in your presence. They're powerless against a tasty crepe.

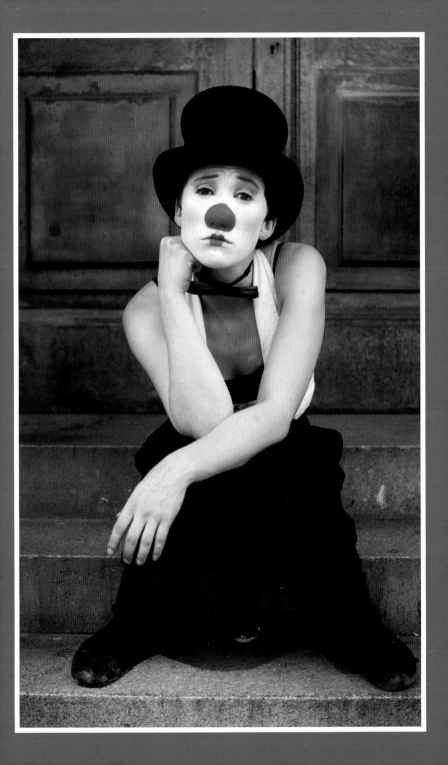

A TALE OF TWO CLOWNS—THE ORIGINS OF CIRQUE DU SOLEIL

The amazing artistic and acrobatic feats that the "clowns" of Cirque du Soleil perform every night are the very definition of everything a "normal" clown loathes—and not just because they can do things a normal clown will never be able to do.

Why such a rift in the clown community?

One need only consult ancient clown mythology to find the answers. As the story goes, it all began in the ancient cradle of clown civilization: Canada. Thousands of years ago, the first clowns emerged from the primordial booze—literally, a cask of bathroom hooch that washed ashore in Labrador (and likely originated in Ireland).

Two clowns grew from this cask—one who was, in today's parlance, a moron, and one who was, also in today's parlance, a pretentious douche. Helpless, confused, and sober, these baby clowns wandered the coastal plains before being discovered by a transient named Brandie Sue. She named the pretentious clown Seth and the fool Randy.

As the brothers grew, their differences began to define them. There was the day a teenaged Seth suddenly showed up dressed all in black and smoking clove cigarettes. There was the day Randy laughed so long and so hard at the duration of a fart that he nearly choked to death.

Seth excelled at magic tricks, balancing acts, reading, and poetry. Randy excelled at wrestling, showstopping flatulence, spitting, and the ability to polish off a fifth of grain alcohol in less than an hour. The brothers soon grew to despise each other and could not agree on where they should build their empire and propagate the clown race.

The years went by, and each began mingling with humans, building up two tribes of like-minded individuals—for Seth, musicians, artists, and contortionists; for Randy, outlaws, fast-food addicts, and one-man bands. The numbers of each tribe grew vast, and they began doing tricks and acts to amuse one another—for Seth, high-wire acts; for Randy, anti-social shenanigans such as the development of the first whoopee cushion.

At last Randy, jealous of the positive reviews his brother's early work garnered in the press, got sloshed on root beer and moonshine, then drunkenly sabotaged one of Seth's shows. The brawl that followed marked the beginning of the brutal thousand-year conflict known as the Clown Wars.

Many of Seth's minions were injured or killed in the vicious fights, and his troupe was all but wiped out. Randy and his followers conquered, thrived, thieved, and drank. Foreseeing the complete annihilation of his kind, Seth and a small number of rebels moved to a city that they subsequently named Quebec. They began speaking French because they believed it made them seem more artistic and refined. Randy's tribe moved to what is now the United States, to a place he named "New Jersey," meaning "New Palace of the Clowns" in the ancient bozo tongue.

Later, Randy took his show on the road. So, too, did Seth, naming his outfit "Cirque du Soleil"—which translates to "Circus of the Sun," a proclamation of shame upon his brother, and a final attempt to display his own superiority.

—ZACHARY PETIT, Mythology Archivist

hat

wig

red nose

weapon

oversized pants

shoes

CLOWN ANATOMY

You ever come across someone on a street corner who won't take their hands out of their pockets? A little red flag goes up in your mind, doesn't it? You wonder what they may be hiding in those pockets. Well, when you come across a clown, it's basically the same feeling multiplied by infinity times a thousand. "Everything a clown wears has the potential to be a weapon," says Miami-Dade Police Sergeant Dwayne Weyland. "The clown's greatest advantage is that he appears unarmed and innocent, but there is more than meets the eye with everything he wears and carries around. If people knew the weapons clowns carried on them at all times, they'd avoid circuses like typhoid."

Before you engage a clown face-to-face or even step outside a guarded area like your home, it's important to understand the anatomy of a clown and how clowns can use costumes and clothing to their advantage in a fight. Here we will break down everything a clown can and will use against you in a brawl.

HAT

Oversized clown hats are just the right size to not only fit a customary flask of booze underneath, but also to hide anything from duct tape to a carton of rotten eggs (clown hair is surprisingly cushioning). The hat cache is nothing new: the annals of history indicate that during Prohibition, more than

22 percent of smuggled hooch was transported underneath the hats of bozos. Also note that a flower on the hat may look harmless, but it could also be weaponized into a device dispensing nitrous oxide or ether. Best case: it squirts skunked water, toxic clown urine, or cheap vodka.

There are many different types of headgear that a clown can employ, but one thing unites all types of joker hats: none of them is what it appears. Consider a few of the most common ones:

The oversized five-, ten-, or fifteen-gallon hat: Even the smaller ones are large enough to hide a Colt .45, a sharpened fork, a second Colt .45, a tarantula, a dime bag of drugs, and more. The largest ones can hide a fold-up unicycle for quick getaways, or a machete for when a quick getaway is not an option.

The beanie (with or without propeller): Since the hat is much too small for the clown, the logical question is "When and where did the clown beat a small person unconscious and steal the hat?" However, if the beanie is not stolen, the propeller may actually double as a ninja star, a glass cutter, or simply a bottle opener to help with the twenty-six Schlitzes the clown consumes in a typical day.

The bowler/derby hat: This hat, which could only have come from a 1922 time warp, makes a clown seem outdated, lost, and confused. In other words, deceptively harmless, which a clown is anything but.

The dunce cap: The dirty secret to this headgear is it's not a "hat" at all, but rather a disguised personal grenade launcher. Plus, the hat is just tall enough to conceal a lock pick used for breaking into nearby cars.

WIG

No clown wig is without its problems. Take the rainbow wig, which can only be described as the illegitimate offspring of an Afro and a box of crayons. But it's not just a poor sartorial choice — it's part of a clown's arsenal. Each ridiculous fiber has the tensile strength of one of Superman's hairs. With a quick yank, the clown, if cornered, has a lethal garroting device, a trip wire, or strong rope with which to hogtie your limbs.

Frequently buried under that mop are *hearing enhancers*, which makes it difficult to sneak up on the bastards. If your goal is to combat and engage a clown, first disable his supersonic auditory senses with a dog whistle. You can even give him a sweet taste of his own medicine; overload that clown hearing aid by using his own air horn on him at close range.

FACE PAINT

A clown's facial makeup is his signature characteristic. For thousands of years, clowns have employed this artifice. A painted face acts as a "mask" and allows the mask wearer to not abide by societal standards. It's a freeing maneuver that allows a person to slip from the world of Normalville into the world of Wacky Bonkers Land. The person becomes anonymous—above the law—and normal rationality slowly starts to slip away, because consequences go out the window. Plus, there's no way you can slather greasepaint on your cheeks day by day and not start to think about it as *war paint*. And when war paint goes on, things can get violent real fast.

We've made great strides of late in learning more about the clown's facial makeup—or, should I say, *protection*. We now know that top-of-the-line greasepaint is fireproof, acid-proof, and pepper spray-proof. And the common addition of Radium 9XZ4—invisible to the naked eye—also renders the clown's face invisible to night vision goggles and scopes. This also makes it nearly imperceptible in dim moonlight.

FACIAL SYMBOLS SCRUTINIZED

A clown composes an assortment of symbols and designs on his face. While these markings may seem to be innocuous and whimsical, BozoWatch director Milos Havel notes they are often used to symbolize clown gang affiliations as well as crimes they've committed in the past. "Just as an ordinary criminal gets a tattoo of an eye tear to symbolize a murder in his past, clowns adopt the same philosophy," Havel says. For example:

+ **A STAR DESIGN** near the eyes symbolizes power and position. These are high-ranking clown mobsters, and a double star (both eyes) is often the sign of a Clownfather who runs the whole show.

+ **BLACK TEARS** below the eyes represent how many silent mimes they've bludgeoned to death. Do not mess with these particular bozos. They're the ones who have done hard time and can fashion a prison shiv out of a balloon.

+ **A SMALL RED SPOT ON THE TIP OF THE NOSE** (in lieu of a large plastic or foam nose) is typically worn by a master hypnotist. Stare at that spot for a surprisingly short period of time and you'll become entranced. That's when the clown takes your Rolex—or worse, a kidney.

+ A clown face with **MULTIPLE RED HEARTS** is a sure sign he's in the sex trade. The heart faces are clown fetish prostitutes for hire, and potentially riddled with STDs. These people are not only good in bed, they're likely budding con artists as well, and very skilled at getting you to reveal your ATM pin code or your house safe combination.

NOSE

The mainstay of any clown face, the large red nose is usually made from foam or latex. A clown's nose is supposed to calm carnival-goers and possibly even bring a little levity with a comedic squeeze or two. But the reality is it just freaks us out. For starters, it's way too big. We associate bulbous red noses with drunks and winos. More important, those ball noses are affixed with high-grade industrial glue, meaning that when clowns are on the job, they are *literally huffing fumes the whole time*. The glue huffing is only part of the drug problem: random testing indicates that 53 percent of all clown noses have tested positive for traces of cocaine. No wonder clowns maintain such high energy levels! This makes them fearless and unpredictable.

SHOES

With their ridiculous size, clown shoes constitute a deadly weapon, according to the statutes in forty-seven U.S. states and more than a hundred countries worldwide. Consider for a moment a scenario in which you're knocked downed by a clown and confront those colossal footwear weapons. "This is what's known as the 'Clown Frown Beatdown,'" says Dr. Ryan McElvy. "Clowns' gigantic footwear not only gives them a menacing appearance but also offers a distinct advantage in any kind of combat."

You've probably already figured out that clowns are fans of wearing bright colors, but did you also know that their shoe color designates their hierarchy in a crime syndicate? It's true. Says FBI Special Agent Chad McWertwill, "For a short while, we had an informant embedded in a Los Angeles clown gang. Before he was discovered and force-fed sno-cones until his stomach ruptured, the informant fed us information—the most valuable of which was his cracking the code on how shoe color determines the clown's place in the crew, much like the color of a martial arts belt is directly relevant to one's skill level."

Here is a breakdown of what the informant told McWertwill:

 Red shoes are worn by "normal" clowns and regular roustabouts. This is why you see so many clowns wearing red. It means he has little to no affiliation or is actively seeking to earn his stripes and attract the attention of a gang.

 Red and yellow shoes are worn by soldiers — clowns on the front lines dealing narcotics, committing felonies, and handling the vice trade.

 Yellow shoes are worn by experienced, ranking clown gangbangers, such as lieutenants and capos.

 Blue shoes are worn by "made men" in the bozo gang. If you look down and see blue on a joker's feet, you're face to face with a person who has likely killed dozens in the course of his decades with the group. Beware.

 White shoes are worn only by clown godfathers. The white shoe was first introduced by clownfather Gondola in 1970s Philadelphia; the symbolism was that his shoes were always immaculate because "nothing could touch him."

OVERSIZED PANTS

Those pants that clowns wear hang off their bodies like the jeans of a person who just lost 250 pounds. This means that when you stand near them, you can *actually see down their pants* without really trying, whether or not they wear ineffective suspenders.

Considering that these pants are almost never washed, it's no surprise they reek of fart and sadness. Each interior-pocketed leg can hold two or three cartons of cigarettes for personal use or prison trade. And if they can stash multiple cartons of smokes, they can easily hide an aluminum bat or a sawed-off shotgun strapped to a thigh.

Moreover, a clown's pants are, in effect, one of his key trophies—every time a clown wins a barfight, he tailors the pants to make them one size larger, adding yet another X to his XXXXXXL outfit. The larger the pants, the greater the cause for alarm.

CLOWN COMMUNICATION & LINGO

Clowns have their own specific language, both verbal and nonverbal. What you read here constitutes the little we know so far about translating clown communication—it's the start of what will be the first public lexicon of "clownspeak." If you hang around circus folk enough, you'll quickly learn to interpret words and phrases like these:

- ✦ **"Sparkle/mule"** (code for *yes* and *no*)
- ✦ **"A big-top guy"** (a standup fellow—a carnie to be taken seriously)
- ✦ **"Dynamite"** (a *mark*, or an easily irritated circus-goer who is egged into a fight for lawsuit purposes)
- ✦ **"Leatherhead"** (a clown pickpocket who specializes in purses and wallets)
- ✦ **"Paint it black"** (an execution assignment for a clown assassin)
- ✦ **"A Rainbo Bright"** (a clown prostitute)
- ✦ **"I need a little fresh air"** (a clown signal that he wants to inhale more nitrous oxide)

Getting familiar with this strange vernacular can save your life. In the heat of the moment, when a clown pulls a weapon, you may think about reasoning with him rather than just handing over your car keys and cash. This is absolutely the worst idea you could have. Ever notice how clowns aren't big talkers? Sure, they guffaw and laugh like dying hyenas, but many are not fond of the spoken word. This is not a coincidence. When clowns are performing in front of an audience (especially in a circus), audience members can't hear them speak. So they've trained for decades to communicate with action and motion, not speech—hence their notable silence.

Even if you find a chatty clown, clownspeak includes a variety of constantly changing, confusing terms and slang. Recently the National Intelligence Center of Spain (Centro Nacional de Inteligencia) released these few confirmed translations—acquired through wiretaps and deciphered by former clowns—to give examples of the evolution of clowns' verbal deception:

"You better get me those ding dongs, or horse feed is all we'll be spinning on these plates for the RC!"

Translation: If we don't find a way to make more money, we'll all be broke and won't have enough to eat for the remainder of the season.

"This roustabout alley-oop just pulled a purple ball fink on the King Pole."

Translation: This contract worker doesn't know how to set up a simple act.

"If you're a gilly spying for a clem, a gaggle of zanies I know would be happy to watch you lick the polka dots."

Translation: If you're an outsider and want to fight, I will assemble a group of armed clowns to kick your ass.

"Zip the pips and hug the mud!"

Translation: There is a rainstorm moving in, so dress appropriately to set up the big top.

"Chances are the squeakiest squeaker needs some noodling off before the blue rubes come tramplin' about."

Translation: Kill the snitch before he rats to the feds.

"Shoot that mime."

Translation: Shoot that mime.

"He took a pony ride to Clowntown."

Translation: A fellow clown has passed away.

"Go love some dung."

Translation: Literally, "Report to the elephant train cars so you can clean up their poop." It's a clown way of saying, "Go to hell." Clowns are notorious for their code of silence when dealing with police, and will often utter only these four words when interrogated.

INFAMOUS CLOWNS

THE JOKER. Batman's most famous nemesis, the Joker is a psychopathic mass murderer who bills himself as the "Clown Prince of Crime." One of his signature elements is a high-pitched squeal of a laugh—which is why we can't take any pleasure when a carnival clown tries a fake laugh in the name of good fun.

RONALD MCDONALD. Ol' Ronald holds a scary place in our hearts because he is likely the first clown we get to know by name when we're impressionable tots. But as we get older, we start to notice that it looks like he copied his hair color from the skin of Satan. His lack of different colors of makeup on his face (too much white) accentuates his red mouth, which reminds us of blood-guzzling vampires. And his outfit? Bright yellow, just like a man waiting to clean up a toxic waste accident. He is not a happy spokesman. He is, in fact, a creator of nightmares.

PENNYWISE, the Dancing Clown from *It*. Pennywise appeared in clown form throughout King's novel—killing people, while also claiming to be "an eater of worlds . . . and children." When the TV adaptation of the book was released in 1990, one-fifth of all the children who watched the show were paralyzed in a drooling, catatonic state of fear for weeks.

KRUSTY THE CLOWN. Krusty, the belligerent clown on *The Simpsons*, personifies one of the major reasons that clowns are awful to be around. We all know they are maudlin, unbalanced people and desperately yearning for attention, yet they continue the charade of jolliness. No sane person cakes his face in makeup and cracks the same jokes to kids a thousand times— that has to be someone hiding deeper dissatisfaction and mental disorders.

RICHARD NIXON. The evidence is there. He officially started National Clown Week with a proclamation, and his memorable face has exaggerated bozo-like features. Take a look at Tricky Dick's schnoz again—it's definitely clown material.

JOHN WAYNE GACY. A fat clown serial killer. While masquerading around town as a party clown named Pogo— because "clowns can get away with murder" (an actual Gacy quote!)—Gacy killed thirty-three teenage boys. When the police dug up the bodies in Gacy's crawl space, exasperated clowns everywhere collectively threw their hands up in the air and said, "Well, that's just *great*."

3

DEFEND

How to Fight Back

BOZO HOTSPOTS

LIKELY LOCATIONS TO SPOT THE ENEMY

The easiest way to avoid getting maimed by a rogue clown is simply to avoid them altogether. And the first step to successful avoidance is understanding where they hang out. Part of the problem is that a clown could be anywhere at anytime, which is why you should always be vigilant. That unfortunate fact aside, there are certainly some bozo-heavy areas to take note of. Stay clear of the following:

THE CIRCUS. I know the trapeze stunts look cool, and the human cannonball is quite a thrill to watch—but for the love of God, don't go to the circus. Four percent of the reason is because they beat the elephants; the other 96 percent is that you'll surround yourself with maniacal clowns who will club your kneecap with a polo mallet just to watch your expression change.

CARNIVALS. Right up there among the most commonsense places to avoid is any kind of traveling carnival. You'll find all kinds of breeds at such a horror show, including the belligerent dunking booth clown. Rural carnival clowns snatch up more children than any of their brethren elsewhere.

CHILDREN'S BIRTHDAY PARTIES. You think you're safe driving around a nice suburb in that fancy Subaru? Think again. Every weekend in your neighborhood, you can bet there's at least one clown performing at a nearby birthday party. Avoid these fiestas like the plague unless you want a contract out on your life after you insult a clown who has deep cartel affiliations.

CLOSED AMUSEMENT PARKS. While you will certainly run into a clown every now and then in an open, functioning amusement park, it is the closed, run-down parks that hold the stuff of nightmares. This is where whacked-out, truly unhinged jokers hang out and permanently live. "Not only do homeless, crazy clowns live at abandoned theme parks, it's also rumored that clowns bury their dead at amusement parks that have shuttered their doors," says Johann Bertlesdorf, author of *The Scariest Places on Earth.* "The last place you want to be is standing on a clown burial ground among clown gravesites. If you are discovered, clown protocol requires that they try to kill you to ensure no loose ends."

ANY PLACE CALLED "THE FUNHOUSE." I don't care if we're talking about an amusement park hall of mirrors or a chicken joint you find off the interstate in Georgia. If the formal name is "The Funhouse," absolutely do not enter unless you really don't mind losing your wallet and/or a pint of blood. Clowns are unconsciously and magnetically drawn to funhouses of any kind, like fish that return to their spawning grounds.

CLOWN COLLEGES. Thankfully, clown colleges are dwindling in number (at least in the United States). It looks like anti-clown efforts to drive up tuition by imposing new taxes on their schools have paid off. But if there is a clown college in your area, keep a one-mile distance from it, and never get on any public transportation that has the college on its route.

RAILROADS. These are hotspots for traveling hobo clowns. Avoid the tracks and stick to brightly lit roads.

DIVE BARS. It's no secret that these big-nosed bastards love a Mai Tai from time to time. And they're not getting drunk at an Applebee's bar. They're getting drunk at hole-in-the-wall joints.

BEHIND YOU AT AN ATM MACHINE. Soft *hyuk-hyuk* laughter is the last thing you'll hear before you get clubbed on the head and black out.

TARGETS FOR ATTACK

WHY YOU SHOULD AVOID CITY HALLS AND STATE CAPITALS

With all this talk about pies flying into people's faces and petty theft, you may have already forgotten that clowns' ultimate goal is *supremacy*—to rule over plainface civilians while enforcing clown law and being the laughingstocks of the world no longer. To achieve this, clowns are slowly laying the groundwork to start their own autonomous nations while also prepping for the worst by transforming their bodies to withstand nuclear fallout. This is a serious threat and cannot be ignored.

In fact, clowns have a history of successfully overthrowing government entities in *coups d'état* and taking control to establish their own rule. Here are some of the most noteworthy clown coups of all time—both successful and not—from around the world:

1582: LONDON. Ballshire the Goof, a prominent court jester of the Tudor dynasty in England, incited what is thought to be the first attempt at a national takeover by clowns. Ballshire was kept under the service of the royal court for jokes and amusement; when his jokes were deemed unsatisfactory, he would be beaten. This is believed to have driven him stark raving berserk, and he responded by bringing two dozen other disgruntled jester types and performers into the royal palace under the guise of putting on a show. Once Ballshire and his cohorts were near the throne room, they killed a few guards and claimed the palace as their own, with Ballshire proclaiming that the nation was "now under Fool's Rule!" To prove their point, the new rulers all collectively mooned London from a tall palace tower. Their alleged first order of business was to deem that all current royals were now their slaves. But before the ragtag group could even locate a quill and ink to write down the land's new "laws," they were arrested by soldiers. The next morning, Ballshire's last words before his execution by hanging were, "Boy, I do love hanging out with my friends in the morning! *Hyuk-hyuk!*"

1819: KASKASKIA, ILLINOIS. This is the first and only verified instance of clowns successfully taking over an entire U.S. state. It was during Kaskaskia's short run as the capital of Illinois that a handful of clowns entered the building and seized control. The following account comes from the *Kaskaskia Sentinel,* the town's largest paper at the time:

> *Vagrant thugs with painted faces raided the government building on the morning of June 16. Some of these men, brandished knives, killed several employees of the capital. While the temporarily victorious intruders yelled, "Now only*

clowns may live in this state!" the remaining government employees quickly escaped unharmed. Shouting out a window, one painted vagrant warned listeners that the state would be flooded with thousands of their kind — who would then kill all nonperformers. However, the vagrants soon became intoxicated and passed out, allowing the armored cavalry to storm the premises and round them up. Their execution by firing squad is scheduled for tomorrow.

1981: Belmopan, Belize. For one week during the fall of 1981, the entire Central American country of Belize was taken over by more than three hundred clowns. With the support of military personnel inside the capital who were bozo sympathizers, the invaders killed seventeen people within minutes of entering the building and took another fifty hostage. The clowns released a list of new "Clown Commandments," with demands such as "Thou shalt always laugh at a clown's buffoonish pun—under pain of death." Arlenn Castillo, the lead hostage negotiator for the Belizean government, later wrote in his memoir how impossible it was to understand the clowns' demands: "Every time I got on the phone to negotiate, before any real conversation could begin, they insisted on no fewer than fifteen knock-knock jokes." Government officials told the clowns that requested commandment was now in place—and that they would have 24/7 access to children's groups simply to perform, as demanded. Minutes later, all three hundred clowns walked out the front door, feeling victorious. "I specifically remember that they kept asking about the children and if we were going to uphold our end of the agreement," Castillo says. "They kept asking right up until the moment our soldiers stuffed them into small clown cars and pushed the locked cars into the ocean."

2003: WINDHOEK, NAMIBIA. The extremely poor African country of Namibia doesn't always have much going for it, but that didn't stop fifty-eight clowns from hijacking the country's capital building with handguns, Frisbees, and Silly String shooters. Once they had control of the building and a state-run TV station, the first three demands were broadcast:

1. All national currency must bear the face of a clown so that people will learn to love and revere us.

2. All school curriculums must teach a yearlong Clown Appreciation class to instill the message that clowns are the greatest performers on Earth.

3. Every citizen must appear before their clown masters and be bombarded with pies, to experience the Pain of the Clowns.

Unfortunately for the polka dot occupiers, a building employee who fled during the occupation saw that many of the jokers' guns were not real, but rather props that, when used, would merely shoot out a BANG! flag. Realizing that few of the clowns had real weapons, Namibian soldiers easily entered the building a short time later and arrested all the perpetrators. The bozos were sentenced to life imprisonment—a fact that both Amnesty International and the World Clowncil decry to this day.

WHEN CLOWNS ATTACK

Plenty of the interactions you may have with a clown at events like the circus, a county fair, or a bat mitzvah party will be nonviolent and do no lasting damage. Many jokers don't seek out physical altercations, but rather thrive on creating discomfort and stealing trinkets, valuables, and prescription pills. But several times in your life, you are bound to find yourself across from a clown who has grander goals in mind for his life—such as a complete takeover of the entire city. Those are the times you'll have no choice but to grapple with a bozo.

There are two classic scenarios that will lead you into a fight:

1. You've accidentally wandered into the clowns' territory or funhouse, and they mistake you for an undercover narcotic officer or competing gang member.

2. At some time in the past you've provoked them or gotten in their way, and they're seeking to even the score.

When cornered, or if they have an agenda, clowns will attack—and possibly leave you with a tag on your toe. And as you should know by now, they have more than cream pies and helium in their armory.

CLOWN WEAPONS (THEIR ARSENAL)

Never expect a bozo to come to a fight empty-handed. These people are trained in the dark arts of the circus, and they use props every day of their lives in order to make a living. Before you ever get into a fight-or-flight situation with clowns, understand what kind of whipped cream and whoopee cushions they'll be packing. Here is a sampling of known clown weapons.

PIES: Sure, they're white, fluffy, and sweet tasting. But they also can blind a person when slammed into a face too quickly. In the 2001 case of *John Miller v. Jammies the Clown,* Miller won a large settlement from the local clown union after a high-speed pie to the kisser detached the retina in one of his eyes and also made him break out in hives, as he was allergic to scrumptious lemon-flavored filling.

STILTS: Stilts are commonly worn by a lookout. This individual will signal to other clowns when they've surveyed the area and spotted an easy mark for pickpocketing.

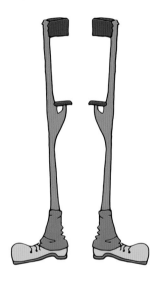

SQUIRTING FLOWER PIN: These pins don't squirt water, my friends. They're much more likely to be filled with harmful or disgusting liquids.

TAINTED JELLY BEANS: Left out for unsuspecting individuals to eat, these goodies are often laced with horse tranquilizers or bath salts. If you accidentally consume the former, you'll pass out, losing your checkbook or perhaps some plasma. If you accidentally consume the latter, you'll go stark raving mad for a short while, and the clowns will gather round to watch you as entertainment. If you ever see a jelly bean trail suspiciously strewn about anywhere, do not follow it.

OVERSIZED MALLET: Self-explanatory. One direct blow to your dome, and your clown-fighting days are over.

Large animals: Just as urban gangs employ pit bulls as guard dogs, clowns use their circus backgrounds to train tigers, bears, and even elephants as protectors. The prospect of fighting off man-eating or man-crushing animals adds a new level of insanity to combat. Do not take on these animals without tranquilizer guns and bear mace on hand.

Air horn: These horns emit a sound that can go up to 150 decibels. The sonic blast stuns and can even deafen. A wily and talented warrior doesn't even need an actual air horn; he knows how to let air slowly escape from a balloon to create a sound that resembles an air raid siren. When people hear it, they head for bomb shelters posthaste, giving nearby clowns a clear path to wreak havoc.

SCARF CHAINS THAT SEEM TO GO ON FOREVER: These can be used to throttle a civilian with ease. An experienced clown can lasso victims from twenty meters away. Even if you're running from a clown, they can hook you from behind. Plus, clown gangs use scarves as a catapult to launch Molotov cocktails against intruding forces or SWAT units.

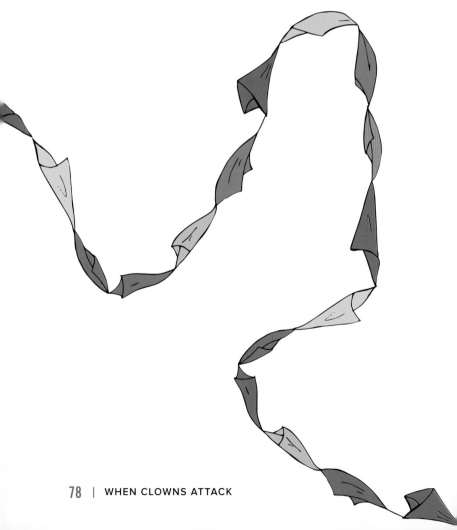

Gas: Because many clowns are addicted to helium or nitrous oxide, some of these jokers have taken it upon themselves to become trained in the art of weaponized gas manipulation. Don't get too close during a fight, or they'll hit you with a puff of self-made "cray-cray fumes," which make you go mad as a hatter. (You'll then willingly join their ranks as a clown soldier, and we all will be discussing how best to put *you* out of commission.)

Exploding cotton candy: When this stuff explodes, it makes napalm look like pop rocks. A sizeable explosion can kill dozens. When you see a clown on the street and he offers you cotton candy as a welcoming gift or act of peace, it's actually a bozo Trojan horse, and you should run the other way.

CANE: Used with specialized clown training, a cane is comparable to the ninja *bō* staff, a deadly martial arts weapon. And many clowns have at least one specially altered cane that flicks out a ricin-laced needle for desperate measures. All clowns also own a "flask cane," which unscrews at the top to hold a half-liter of grain alcohol mixed with root beer—the drink of choice for men of the paint.

RUBBER CHICKEN: Perfect for violently smacking a passerby. Because rubber chickens are so inherently funny, this always gets laughed off, even if it knocks out a few teeth. *No* charges have ever stuck for assault with a rubber chicken, in any court worldwide. Instead, the moment more often simply goes viral on YouTube. (This is now a meme known as "rubber-chickening," just giving the bozos more reason to pop unsuspecting strangers in the face with hopes of achieving internet fame.)

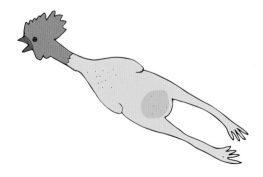

ELECTRIC HAND BUZZER: You think you're simply shaking a gracious clown's hand; you're actually about to be hit with up to a thousand volts of heart-stopping evil. The electric surge momentarily debilitates you, and you're defenseless against theft, molestation, or in some cases, being used as a prop in one of their shows.

WHOOPEE CUSHIONS: There was an incident in 2001 in which clowns placed several whoopee cushions in a movie theater. When moviegoers sat on the cushions, they were amused at the funny noises—but a powerful sedative gas was released from inside. Everyone in the theater passed out. The clowns stole every wallet before hightailing it out of there. The audience woke up just in time to watch the ending of a pointless French film short.

JUST ABOUT ANYTHING ELSE: The scary thing about a clown is that he can make *anything* into a murder weapon. According to Interpol and other law enforcement agencies, the following items have been used by clowns in deadly ways: Rice Krispies to the face, cherry sno-cones, pool flotation noodles, a box of rigatoni, and a stale loaf of bread.

CLOWN ASSAULT TACTICS

If you are attacked by clowns, it's important to know who you're dealing with and what to expect. First of all, stay calm. Second, never further goad or taunt a clown. These people are mentally unhinged, and no good can come from messing with a crazy person. Here are some of the most frequent aggressive clown strategies:

THEY ATTACK IN GROUPS. If they are on the hunt and intend to harm, they rarely will strike solo, unless heavily armed. The bozos will swarm you like a pack of angry fire ants and stomp the bejeezus out of you. And even if you do happen to luck out and square off one-on-one with a lone zany, do not think the odds will be fair for long. According to researcher Kaylon, "It sounds crazy, but our biological testing proves that when a clown is attacked, his body releases a hormone that alerts other nearby clowns—much the same as when you crush a killer bee. "Evidently, the average clown has worn so much greasepaint on his face that alarming levels have seeped into his bloodstream. So when you injure a clown to the point of his bleeding, other clowns can actually 'smell' or 'sense' the blood–facepaint compound from up to a mile away." This means you can certainly clock a clown in the mouth and fight him (you'll have to, in order to survive!), but once he's down for the count, don't stick around. Leave immediately, because a clown army could show up in minutes.

THEY HAVE AN EXCESSIVE NUMBER OF WEAPONS ON HAND.
See pages 74–82.

THEY ARE CLEARLY WHACKED OUT ON DRUGS. According to former clown Doodle (who became a male stripper and renounced clowning altogether), clowns gas up heavily before a fight. Doodle says, "Whenever we would go out for group brawls, most of us would inhale copious amounts of nitrus oxide. First of all, this dulled our senses, so we would become better assets in a battle. Secondly, it was just fun to laugh our asses off! Intense. Good times, actually."

THEY SEND AN ATTRACTIVE CLOWN TO SEDUCE YOU. Picture this, gents. You're in a run-down neighborhood with broken unicycles and three-wheelers nearby. It's getting dark. Things don't look good. Then out of the shadows steps a buxom clown girl who bats her über-long eyelashes and twirls her polka dot umbrella in your direction—giving you that "come hither" motion with her pointer finger. Think it's too good to be true? It is. This sexy "Rainbo Bright" is obviously a trap set by gangster bozos in an attempt to lure you into a local funhouse lair. And men aren't the only ones targeted in such a scheme. Clown gangs are known to keep a handsome, fit male with a six-pack in their ranks. He's usually the one going shirtless, with rainbow suspenders against his lightly oiled, suntanned chest. Run from him.

HOW TO DEFEAT A CLOWN

Now we come to the crucial instructions. If by chance you find yourself matched up with a lone joker who has been separated from his pack, then it's time to quickly engage and defeat with extreme prejudice. Make no mistake—this is a real duel, and your life is on the line right now. When you step up and start the battle, there are right and wrong ways to fight. Know them, so you can take down the clown and score a small victory for all mankind. We'll teach you how to attack effectively, so you can not only take down your opponent, but also flee the area before reinforcements arrive.

WRONG: Try to hit him in the midsection or groin. The midsection area is often padded and disguised by oversize pants. You'll never penetrate that outer casing accurately. A likely scenario is that your punch actually bounces off his belly and ricochets back to tag you in the chin. Also, and I know this may sound strange, *don't* aim for the groin. Doing so will only prompt a humiliating *BOING!* spring noise and a prompt spray of urine from the clown's flower pendant.

RIGHT: Hit him in the face. The face is relatively unprotected and unpadded. You might get some makeup on your knuckles if you do this right, but that's OK.

If he covers his face in defense, punch the liver, which in most clowns is immediately under the right pec. You may have to hit hard enough to break a rib. All that drinking has taken its toll, and clowns develop liver disease ten times quicker than nonclowns. That means there's a good chance your solid right hook to the body can pack a mean wallop.

Right!

WRONG: Stomp on the shoes. Consider the flabbergasting size of the shoes themselves. There's no telling where the foot ends and the empty pleather or plastic begins. Plus, the shoes could be steel-tipped. You easily can break your own foot trying to stomp the clown's. Some clown shoes are even spring-loaded in front, intended to propel the stomper into a backward flip-and-fall.

RIGHT: Kick him in the knee. A solid kick to the kneecap will cripple a clown soldier and drop him right to the ground. Do this kick right and the clown will be in so much pain that he won't be able to say a word; instead, he'll resort to Clown Rule #10 and hold up a sign with the word *OW!* on it.

WRONG: Fight fair. A clown isn't going to play straight with you, so don't give him an advantage.

RIGHT: Fight dirty. If you have a chance to sucker punch a string bean clown half your size, go for it. Do everything the clown would do to you if given the chance. Hit him when he's not looking. Don't wait for a clown to turn around before you smash that antique vase over his head. Convince a clown that you must both bow to each other prefight, like ancient warriors — but when he bows, you'll roundhouse him in the face. You should take any opportunity to strike, especially when he seems unprepared.

WRONG: Fight fire with fire. When one thinks of a classic duel, it usually involves equally armed opponents — two people, both armed with pistols, or with rapier blades. This type of "everyone is equal" showdown is exactly what you *don't* want. Forget the bro code — you're dealing with a *violent clown.* Please explain to me how, if you both show up with rubber chickens for a duel, the clown won't win? Would you fight a katana duel with a samurai? No. So don't bring some juggling balls to a clown fight.

RIGHT: Bring *better* weapons. He brought some pies? You pull out a Louisville Slugger that has nails in the barrel. He brought some exploding cotton candy? You bust out the mace (but not the pepper spray — their face paint is a protectant). He pulls out a colored scarf lasso? Compliment him on his fashion sense, then show him your bazooka.

CLOWN GANGS

Very little is known about clown gangs, because members are extraordinarily loyal to their own kind. Plus, if gang members do squeal, they are subject to torture, so very few cooperate with law enforcement groups. However, over the years little snippets of informant information have given us some small-but-valuable insights into these gangs. Here's what we know (or *think* we know):

1. Just like with the mafia, it is not individuals but *families* that control some major cities. For example, the Honkers run Dallas, Texas; the Bangarangs control Auckland, New Zealand; and the Petunias have a death grip on vice in São Paulo, Brazil.

2. The bigger and more successful the gang, the more wild animals they will have on headquarters property — for both amusement and warfare.

3. These days, the gangs' growing revenue streams include helium and party balloon sales, ecstasy trafficking, and clown fetish acts.

4. An "independent" is a clown who has no affiliation. Established gangs typically do not trust independents (at least at first) for fear they might be a spy or police plant.

5. Gang turf is a place of no rules, no cops, and no lawsuits. All conflicts are dealt with in-house. Clowns who call the cops or a lawyer are kicked out of the "family" immediately. One account of a discovered clown informant had the snitch walking across a wobbly tightrope over a pit of black mambas while the other jokers took bets on when he'd fall. (The winning bet was on minute two.)

6. When a new Italian mafia member commits his first felony, it's called "making your bones." In clown groups, the comparable expression used is "farting sawdust." On a similar note, a fresh addition to the group is known as a "new nose."

7. As if clowns didn't drink enough to begin with, gangs force their members to consume alcohol in surprisingly large quantities, each and every day. This may be because heavy drinking over time causes nerve damage, and a clown who doesn't feel pain is a valuable weapon in street battles. This is also why you should never attempt to best a clown in a drinking contest. You will lose.

8. Gangs poach from local circuses and juggling schools. Clowns look for talented circus individuals with authority or behavioral problems, then lure them into the fold.

Again, it should be stated that anti-clown task forces are well aware that we have only scratched the surface concerning how circus gangs operate. That's probably why, as this book went to press, the FBI had upped its reward for insider clown gang information to an astonishing $25,000. Even though that kind of serious cash will buy a lot of balloons, so far there have been no takers, says a bureau spokesperson.

> **"To be a clown is to go against the idea of normal. Any moron who wears a U-shaped 'balding' wig if they're already bald is out of their mind—period."**
>
> **— RANDOLPH YAVIN, former clown**

HOW TO ESCAPE A CLOWN POSSE

As we said at the outset, if you are confronted by a solo clown, the tactics in "How to Defeat a Clown" (pages 87–92) can be effective. If confronted by a clown posse, however, or if you are caught unprepared, do *not* be a hero. Your best option is to *not fight*. You're likely outnumbered or outmaneuvered before the first pie is thrown. Here are some suggestions on how to escape without getting brutally murdered:

RUN UP STAIRS. Just take a look at clowns' shoes. Most of the oversized toe portion is hollow, which means it's impossible for a clown to ascend stairs with any grace or speed. He must turn his shoes sideways to climb steps without falling. Even trekking up the side of a hill is a chore in those size 24s. So whenever you can, go up.

JUMP INTO WATER. Because of clowns' oversized clothes, accessories, and weighty flair, if they jump into a pond they will quickly sink to the bottom. Also, water washes off a clown's makeup. If that happens, he ceases to be a full clown—taking away his anonymity and circus "identity"—and therefore removing a significant portion of his power, not to mention protection against pepper spray.

THROW BANANA PEELS. You must always remember that these bozos will never break Clown Law #3. This means if you toss a banana peel at oncoming clowns, some or all *must* step on it. Your hope is that several sprain something in the fall or just plain knock themselves out.

TOSS INVISIBLE OBJECTS when nothing else is available. This is Clown Rule #4.1. If you don't have banana peels or juggling balls (which they will then have to juggle), toss an invisible ball high up in the air and yell, "Catch!" According to the Bozo Doctrine of 1934 set forth by SnuggleJugs the hobo clown, any clown within earshot will have to try to catch the "ball" as it comes down. Not only will this buy you valuable time, but there is also a chance that clowns will bump into one another while trying to catch the ball, incapacitating a few bozos with concussions.

MAKE A FART NOISE OR OTHER JUVENILE SOUND. Clowns are hardwired to laugh at or the lowest common form of humor. They will often double over in giggles at any flatulence sound, real or imitation, giving you valuable time to escape. Also note that armpit farts are worth trying: with about 20 percent of clowns, this triggers a glee so thorough that they may forget about or abandon their attack altogether.

RUN FROM THREE-WHEELERS; DISABLE UNICYCLES. Clowns like to pursue their victims on a comically undersized three-wheeler. If this happens to you, do not panic. The truth is that they can go

only about four miles an hour on those junkers. You can outrun them easily. Unicycles are a different matter. Jokers can travel 75 mph riding the one wheel, but their balance is precarious and the vehicle is vulnerable to sabotage. Just shove or shove a stick into the spokes, and the chase is off.

TAKE ADVANTAGE OF HOT WEATHER. Clowns in full costume are wearing an awful lot of gear, and they get hot very quickly. If you can get them running around for long enough on a hot summer day, their makeup will sweat into their eyes and blur their vision. Even better, they're bound to eventually pass out from heat stroke, allowing you to make a clean getaway.

PULL DOWN THEIR PANTS. If you're up close with a joker fighting for your life, grab his pantaloons and pull. The suspenders are usually cheap, and the pants will easily fall to the floor. The "pants falling down" gag is a clown favorite, so he will have no choice but to enjoy the moment and look around, "embarrassed," before he "blushes." These precious seconds may be enough for you to escape with your jaw intact.

KEEP MOVING. If you stop to negotiate with a clown gang, they will quickly encircle you in their large numbers. And once you go down, there is no getting back up. Also, try to avoid running into a corner or any location without multiple exits. If you do run up to a high floor, make sure you find a safe way down. Remember, clowns can jump from a dizzying height and survive by landing in a small pail of water. You probably cannot.

HOW TO SURVIVE A TRIP TO THE CIRCUS IN THREE EASY STEPS

1. Lock your car keys in a safe.
2. Forget the combination.
3. Don't f**king go.

4

PROTECT

*Evaluate and
Fortify*

The first step to living another day is simply avoiding clowns as much as possible. But steering 100-percent clear of their ilk is a virtual impossibility. In this section, we'll teach you how to identify clowns who hide in plain sight, how to clown-proof your home from intruding bozos, how to recognize when your neighborhood is targeted by clown gangs, and much more.

■ SPOTTING THE PLAINCLOTHES CLOWN ■

The unidentified *plainclothes clown* may be the most dangerous of all jokers, as you rarely know when you're talking to a scary camouflaged performer. Watch what you say to strange people! You could be revealing key anti-clown-attack defense techniques to a circus spy.

Perhaps you nonchalantly mention your upcoming vacation to that "nice guy" at the convenience store—but *oh, wait*—yep, he's a card-carrying bozo. So when you disappear for that trip the whole family's pumped about, he and his dirty circus buddies plow through your unguarded front door. Say good-bye to your valuables, your alcohol, and your ability to have another night of peaceful sleep.

The good news is that plainclothes clowns can't help but give themselves away with many clues that reveal their true identity. Here are some things to look for:

RASHES ON THE CHEEKS, FOREHEAD, AND NECK. Although a few plainclothes clowns never don the paint, most do, and these individuals will develop rashes in these areas from wearing makeup and wigs in the heat.

POSSESSING AN ABUNDANT SUPPLY OF MEDIOCRE JOKES. If the guy is happy to rattle off ten minutes of puns and jokes without stopping to breathe, he's a damn clown.

AVERSION TO OR HATRED OF A BERET. A black beret is the international symbol of the mime, a clown's sworn enemy. If you're wearing a beret in the local supermarket and notice that the cashier has been giving you an evil eye for ten minutes straight (and it just so happens all her fingernails are painted in different colors and her nametag says "Jubilee"), then, *bingo,* she's *inclownito.*

VAST AMOUNTS OF TWINKIES IN THE HOME. If you visit someone and see an odd abundance of Twinkies on hand, then I suggest you run away across the country, change your name, and live a quiet life under your new identity because you've just run into an absolute insanely hardcore clown. Remember that the ultimate goal of bozos is to create their own clown-only societies, and Twinkies are a key tactic for surviving a nuclear blast. Because Twinkies are thought to be capable of withstanding thermonuclear war, all clowns are encouraged to

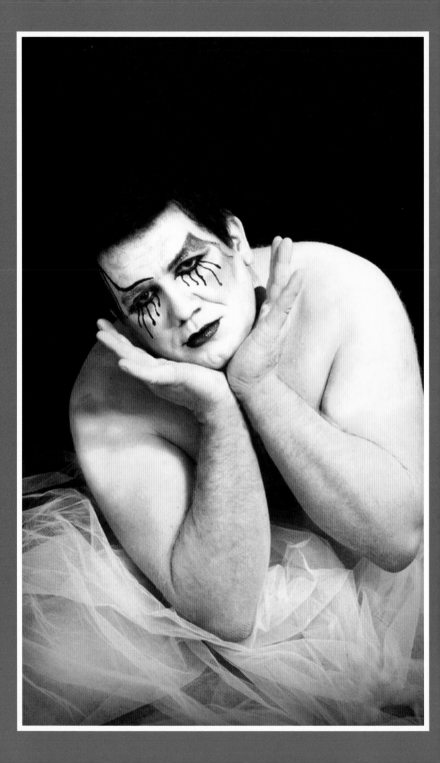

stuff themselves with the sweet treats to adapt their bodies to withstand high levels of radiation.

IN-DEPTH KNOWLEDGE OF MAKEUP. If you suspect that an acquaintance is a clown, contact him via social media or email and say you're confused about the difference between blush and bronzer, or kohl and gel eyeliner—you get the idea. A clown can't help but blurt out the answer with relish. Have this conversation via social media (rather than phone) so you can easily take a screenshot of the conversation to use as evidence at his criminal trial.

ALWAYS PERFORMING. Clowns are showmen at heart, and that is something that never gets out of their blood. They're the ones trying out their new "one-man band" disaster of an idea at the local farmer's market. They're the ones playing Santa Claus in their later years. If there's a guy at work who's always "on," make a mental note of him and stay clear.

A HATRED OF ANIMAL RIGHTS ACTIVISTS. Because People for the Ethical Treatment of Animals (PETA) airs hidden videos of animal abuse under the big top, the organization is the mortal enemy of circus folk everywhere. If you bring up how you're going to stop wearing real fur because of sympathy for animals, and a friend of yours reacts almost violently to your decision, that's a plainclothes red flag all the way.

Sideshow skills. If you begin to talk about oddball sideshow abilities such as hula-hooping or serving as a human blockhead, beware of anyone who replies, "I can do that!!" with a straight face. Clowns are consummate braggarts, and they can't help but give themselves away in situations like these.

The need to mouth off and answer questions with a question. Clowning is a rough gig, and over time clowns become belligerent, unlikeable boobs. Although they can take off their makeup and act polite, the prickly edge always remains. If you ask someone to lend you a dollar and he gently says, "Sorry, no," that means he's not a clown. If you ask someone to lend you a dollar and he says, "What am I — a bank? What is this — Wall Street?", then you may well be talking with a disguised bozo.

Unexplained enthusiasm for the circus. An obvious point, sure, but an important one nonetheless.

Abrupt appearance with "adopted" kid(s). Remember, because of a lack of female equivalents to reproduce with, male clowns often must abduct youngsters to propagate their race. If a buddy of yours on the company softball team just happens to keep "adopting" kids every summer weekend the circus happens to be in town, it's time to start looking at the backs of milk cartons to match those faces with his new kids.

Any image of St. Genesius. If you see this saint on a home or office wall, be on high alert. He is the patron saint of clowns, and his presence signals that you're within stilt's reach of a crazy joker.

WORD ASSOCIATION TEST

When he was nine years old, a Greek boy named Loxias Theodokos was scared into a coma by a menacing Athens clown. Though he recovered, Loxias never forgot the incident. Upon reaching a prominent position with Greece's largest security agency in the late 1990s, he developed the now well-known Clown Word Association Test, designed to draw out plainclothes jokers who are hiding in plain sight. The test is now used by security officials worldwide. Here is Loxias's testing lexicon:

CONTROL WORLD	DANGEROUS RESPONSE WORDS/ PHRASES
Big	Top
	Nose
	Pants
	Fall
Three	Rings
Balloon	Animals
	Performer
Car	Crowded
	Honk-honk
Mimes	Die
	Kill
	Scum
Love	Circus
	Clowns
	Being a clown

COMMON CLOWN HEALTH PROBLEMS

After decades of debauchery and antics, clowns develop an assortment of ailments specific to their lifestyle. While any individual anywhere can have one of the following conditions, a combination of four or more is a sure diagnosis of a retired clown in hiding.

GLAUCOMA: A result of one too many lemon meringue pies straight into the peepers.

KYPHOSIS ("HUNCHBACK"): A result of being stuffed into uncomfortable positions in clown cars for God knows how long.

OSTEOARTHRITIS OF THE FEET: A result of no proper shoe support. Evidently those plastic monstrosities they call footwear come back to bite you in the ass after all.

DEMENTIA: A result of huffing too many fumes from makeup and bus diesel.

ULCER: A result of many severe stressors, including (but not limited to) constant gang warfare with civilians or other troupes of jokers, and being in witness protection after ratting on fellow bozos.

CIRRHOSIS OF THE LIVER: A result of way too much alcohol consumption.

DIABETES: A result of way too much sugar consumption.

SPINAL DISC HERNIATION: A result of too many pratfalls, many of which involve bad landings on hard surfaces.

HEARING LOSS: A result of enthusiastic five-year-old circus-goers blowing air horns in the clown's ear as he approaches.

SIGNS THAT CLOWNS ARE NEARBY

If your home sits on the edge of circus territory, you'll be warned early and often. Clowns don't like unwelcome guests in their neighborhood unless you're a paying customer at a circus — and even then you're not completely safe. Here are some of the many indicators that experts look for when trying to determine which city blocks are under clown gang control.

CIRCUS GRAFFITI. Clowns mark walls and bridge underpasses with spray-painted symbols of unicycles, balloon giraffes, and dead mimes. Such tagging can be in any color but is most often in red and yellow, the traditional colors of the big top.

SIGNATURE MUSIC. This includes so-called "circus music" (calliope music and "screamers") as well as accordion melodies and oompah tuba tunes. If you hear this music, you know a bad encounter is about to happen.

THE SOUND OF SQUEAKY SHOES. This wettish *fwapping* noise is made by a clown trailing you, inadvertently giving away his position through the echoing clomps of his footwear. You may not see him yet, but start looking for escape routes or a weapon.

LOTS OF MUD AND/OR ANIMAL POOP. Circuses perform in fields, so they must constantly deal with mud. For you or me, mud is a dirty nuisance. But to clowns, mud is a reminder of home; that's why they purposefully muddy up fields and backyards. Also, where you find clowns, you find big circus animals. And those creatures don't crap rainbows, my friend. Following large-ish animal dung clues will likely lead you straight to a clown lair, which is never a place you want to be.

CIRCUS SMELLS. These commonly include buttered popcorn, diesel exhaust, animal feces, and sawdust. Add to any of those a scent of used clothing (that "thrift store smell"), and you're no doubt close to Clownburg. By the way, thrift stores are like second homes to bozos; they love to pick up cheap, oversized outfits. Be very careful when shopping in these.

SOUND OF DEMENTED LAUGHTER. Much as a rattlesnake makes noise before it strikes, clowns have an unconscious compulsion to hoot before they strike. If you hear the deadly *hyuk-hyuk* sounds, it's already too late to plan a counterattack. Make a run for it!

EMPTY ENERGY DRINK CONTAINERS. News flash: clowns are drunks! They imbibe alcohol a lot, and drinking saps your energy—but this is a problem for them, because clowns need to be high-energy dervishes all the time. Their solution is to constantly consume *both* alcohol and high-caffeine energy drinks to keep themselves both drunk and manic—a perfectly horrifying combination. According to the FBI, recently clowns have even succeeded in perfecting a "peppy cocktail" that is supposed to be five times more potent than regular energy drinks. (Jokers affectionately call this "clown hooch.")

RAILROADS. Old-school clowns, such as hobo clowns and elderly mafioso types, insist on traveling by train because that's the way they did it back in the day. If you ever ask a clown for directions (though there would be no sane reason to do this), he will give you directions via the railroad, with every path involving "walking along the tracks, whistling a tune" for a while.

Also beware clown-controlled cities that have deep ties to the circus. These include Baraboo, Wisconsin (the Circus World Museum); Delevan, Wisconsin (the International Clown Hall of Fame); Peru, Indiana (the International Circus Hall of Fame); Sarasota, Florida (the largest clown college in the nation); and wherever you see a renaissance fair playing.

CLOWN ALLIES

Unless proven otherwise, assume that all individuals who participate in the circus or carnivals are clown allies and therefore cannot be trusted. "The circus is one big family of weirdos," says Morris Potter, founder of the pro-safety, anti-clown site, ClownsKillPeople.com. "All those who work under the big top are loyal to each other and would happily take a whiskey bottle to your head before giving up one of their own."

DO NOT TRUST: aerialists, animal trainers, bearded ladies, carnies, jugglers, ringmasters, pro-clown groups, puppeteers, sword-swallowers, trapeze artists, tumblers, wirewalkers, and strong men.

Then there are the groups of people we don't yet know whether to trust. The jury is still out on these "cousins" of a sort.

UNCERTAIN TRUSTWORTHINESS: Blue Man Group, clown-painted musicians (such as Insane Clown Posse and KISS), dummies and their ventriloquists, Siamese twins, and clownfish.

And finally, we come to the sworn enemies of clowns. These are the people you want to cozy up to immediately.

ALWAYS TRUST: Animal rights activists, PETA, mimes, Cirque du Soleil, and Daughters of the American Revolution. And Matt Damon. You can always trust Matt Damon.

PROTECT YOUR HOME

Avoiding any clown-heavy areas such as carnivals is just the beginning of ensuring your safety. You'll need to do more. In the last decade, these painted warriors have started a proactive assault on our homes — either to acquire children and valuables, or to end the life of a federal witness. If you have slighted a clown or observed one of their crimes, then consider yourself a high-risk target. But even low-risk targets should be ready for a bozo home invasion. And when the jokers come for you and yours (and they will), it won't be just one; the whole troupe will bang down the door in an explosion of party poppers. A fence won't help; they'll just use a trampoline to bound over it.

Here are some quick tips on how to fortify and defend your home both before and when they come.

LOCK YOUR WINDOWS. Sure, people know to lock their ground-floor windows, but they aren't as diligent about locking the ones upstairs as well. Clowns will climb nearby trees using their long strands of scarves and throw a grappling hook onto your roof. They can skillfully walk across this makeshift tightrope, and from there, it's just a few steps to the open window.

SET OUTDOOR TRAPS: If you think the painted ones will come for your children, they no doubt *will*, so start setting up hidden defensive measures on your property. The best way is to dig a deep hole in the ground—ten feet is a good start. Conceal it with some sticks and leaves. On top of the trap, place a tray of delicious funnel cakes and corndogs—because lord knows a joker cannot possibly resist tasty carnival food. Once he takes the deep-fried bait, he'll fall into the pit and be trapped until law enforcement arrives.

PLAN FOR ANIMALS, TOO. If you face a full-on bozo onslaught, realize that they'll throw the kitchen sink at your home in an attempt to breach your defenses, including animals. Monkeys, tigers, bears, and elephants are frequently kept and used by jokers during their home offensives. The best way to keep the animals distracted is to have food at the ready. Throw peanuts at the elephants; toss steaks at the tigers; and just shoot the psycho monkey with a gun (you'll be driven mad by the clash of those little cymbals).

STOCKPILE WEAPONS. You won't get far fighting back with coat hangers and couch cushions, so I suggest packing some serious armaments in your house, including, but not limited to handguns, rifles, machetes, aluminum softball bats, Scottish long swords, maces, battle axes, and spears.

KEEP YOUR STAIRS MESSY. We already know that fat shoes make it tough for clowns to ascend stairwells. But you should also remember that the more doggie chew toys and children's wheeled toys you have lying around, the more the intruder can

step on and fall, making amusing "OW! OOO! EEE! YOWZA!" sounds the whole way down.

HAVE A CIRCUS MUSIC CD READY TO GO. If the back door gets smashed to smithereens and you find yourself in a life-or-death clown fight, one of the best things you can do is start a prearranged playlist that blares up-tempo circus music. The clowns will instinctually go into dance routines and joke sketches. It will take them at least of 120 seconds for them to break out of their trance-dance, giving you valuable escape time.

ASSEMBLE A "SCARECLOWN" IN YOUR FRONT YARD: Create an improvised scarecrow designed to spook off the jokers. To do this, make the scareclown resemble the person a clown fears most: an asylum worker. After all, a clown's greatest fear is not death but being locked up in a loony bin forever. If a bozo approaches your front yard and sees a psych hospital worker, he'll no doubt turn tail and head back home.

USE ANYTHING SILLY YOU CAN FIND TO BATTLE. A clown is hardwired to believe that whenever the conflict is "clown versus silly object," the silly object must be taken seriously. So even if you hit a clown with a spatula, he'll flail backward in an attempt to get a laugh. Have flour, talcum powder, or some other fine dusty matter at hand? Blow it at him. He'll have to sneeze at least six times. It's always smarter to fight with a silly household item than use your fists. The only exception is a rubber chicken. Clowns are the masters of Kung Pow Chicken.

CONSTRUCT A PANIC ROOM. When the clowns breach your defenses and enter your home, there will be a moment — *there will always be this moment* — when you realize that hope of holding the line is futile, and it's time to simply save yourself and your family. At this moment, you will have nowhere to go unless you have taken this essential precaution: a nearby fully functioning safe room with steel walls and a door of bullet-resistant Kevlar. Once you're safe inside the panic room, use a secure phone line to contact the authorities, then get on the house intercom and say "*Nyah nya nya nyah nyahhh!*" to the clowns.

LIVE NEXT TO COPS — OR BETTER YET, SOME MIMES. Living close to a police officer does a good job of keeping these wackos at bay, but an even better option is to purchase property in a mime-heavy cul-de-sac. As long-time nemeses of clowns, mimes are dedicated to supporting the anti-bozo movement. This means if your house comes under attack from an armada of red noses, a swarm of ninja-like silent soldiers will come to your aid to kick clown ass.

CONTINUE TO WATCH YOUR BACK. Even if you scare the clowns off, you're not safe. The whole *hyuk-hyuk* gang may return another night to try again. Take every precaution you can to fortify your

home, build up your arsenal of weapons, and fight back (to the death, if need be).

WRITE YOUR ELECTED OFFICIALS AND THINK LONG TERM. Sure, keeping your home safe is just dandy. But what happens years from now when clown numbers have increased tenfold? We're all screwed, that's what. Which is why we need to take action *now* to disrupt their lifestyle with the goal of eliminating clowning altogether. For starters, bang on your mayor's door and demand that clowning be illegal in your city. When that's done, donate to U.S. Senator Pamela Riba, sponsor of the Clown Registration Act, a bill stuck in committee that would force current and former clowns to disclose their residence and activities.

CONCLUSION

So now you know everything there is to know about combating a clown. But besides protecting yourself, be sure to inform your friends and family about the real threats and goals of crazy clowns. They'll thank you later. We, meanwhile, thank you *now* for joining the anti-clown movement and educating yourself.

ACKNOWLEDGMENTS

In 1990, I saw the television adaptation of the novel *It*, and had nightmares for years, so I guess that means I need to first thank both Stephen King and Tim Curry for their contribution to this book.

Besides those two, it was several women who were key in this guide coming to life. My agent Sorche Fairbank believed in the work in the beginning. My editor Kaitlin Ketchum is dynamite and hilarious. My designer Tatiana Pavlova made these pages come to life. Ten Speed's Julie Bennett said yes to this idea when it was just my nonsensical mad ravings about killer clowns planning a master community clown-topia. My wife Bre's love and support have been tremendous throughout, as always. And I've just been told by my daughter Geneva that I need to thank her, as well. So thank you, Geneva, for being so cute when you demand things.

Also deserving thanks are my writing friends Brian A. Klems and Zachary Petit, both of whom helped in the rewriting process. And finally, a special thanks to everyone involved in all the images that ended up in the book—from the photographers to the models to the makeup artists. Your pictures are an invaluable contribution to this book, so thank you.

PHOTO CREDITS

Photography credits appear on page 129

Library of Congress Cataloging-in-Publication Data

Sambuchino, Chuck.
When clowns attack : a guide to the scariest people on earth / by
Chuck Sambuchino. — First edition.
        pages cm
1. Clowns — Humor. I. Title.
PN6231.C554S26 2015
791.3'3 — dc23
2015003743

Hardcover ISBN: 978-1-60774-703-1
eBook ISBN: 978-1-60774-704-8

Printed in China

Design and illustrations by Tatiana Pavlova

10 9 8 7 6 5 4 3 2 1

First Edition